MASTERING BUDGETING: A BEGINNER'S GUIDE TO FINANCIAL SUCCESS

By following this comprehensive guide, beginners will gain the knowledge, tools, and confidence needed to create and maintain an effective budget, paving the way toward financial success and security.

INTRODUCTION:

In a world where financial stability and freedom are paramount, the ability to navigate the complex landscape of personal finance is an essential skill. Many of us have felt the weight of financial stress at one point or another—whether it's struggling to make ends meet, drowning in debt, or simply feeling uncertain about our financial future. The good news is that you hold the power to transform this narrative. Welcome to "Mastering Budgeting: A Beginner's Guide to Financial Success."

Consider this book your compass, designed to guide you through the intricate journey of budgeting—an art and science that can reshape your financial reality. Regardless of your background, income level, or previous financial experience, the principles you'll uncover here have the potential to revolutionize the way you manage your money.

Budgeting isn't just about spreadsheets and numbers; it's a powerful tool that empowers you to take control of your financial destiny. With the right knowledge and approach, you can become the master of your money, rather than its captive.

In this guide, we'll peel back the layers of budgeting, starting with the fundamentals. We'll address the misconceptions and fears that often surround the topic, and we'll show you how budgeting is not only achievable but can also be surprisingly freeing.

From understanding your current financial situation and setting goals to crafting a budget that reflects your priorities, you'll learn the practical steps to shape your financial path. We'll delve into the various budgeting methods and tools available, equipping you with the knowledge to choose the approach that suits your style.

Budgeting isn't a one-size-fits-all solution, and we understand that. Life is dynamic, and your financial journey will have its twists and turns. That's why we'll discuss common challenges you might encounter and provide strategies to overcome them.

We'll explore the art of saving and smart spending—how to build that essential emergency fund and make mindful choices when it comes to expenses. We'll also dive into the realm of debt management and credit improvement, showing you how budgeting can be a potent ally in your financial transformation.

But this journey doesn't stop at managing the present. Together, we'll chart a course for your future by delving into long-term financial planning and investing. We'll discuss the road to financial independence and guide you on setting goals that extend beyond immediate needs.

As you embark on this journey of "Mastering Budgeting," remember that every step you take toward financial awareness and control is a step toward a brighter future. The skills you acquire and the habits you develop will not only impact your bank account but also ripple into other areas of your life, providing you with the confidence and resources to pursue your dreams.

So, let's begin. Whether you're new to budgeting or seeking to refine your skills, the insights within these pages will empower you to reshape your financial destiny. Get ready to embark on a transformative journey—one that has the potential to lead you to lasting financial success.

CHAPTER 1: BUILDING A STRONG FOUNDATION

Money matters. It's a statement that holds true for everyone, regardless of age, background, or circumstance. Whether you're fresh out of college, settling into a career, or approaching retirement, the role of money in our lives is undeniable. In this chapter, we'll lay the groundwork for your budgeting journey by focusing on building a strong foundation—because every successful financial journey begins with a solid base.

Understanding Personal Financial Goals and Aspirations

Financial goals are like the North Star that guides your financial decisions and actions. They provide purpose and direction to your financial journey. Before you can effectively manage your money, it's crucial to have a clear understanding of your financial goals and aspirations.

Start by asking yourself:

a) What do I want to achieve financially in the short term (1-3 years), medium term (3-5 years), and long term (5+ years)?
b) Are there specific financial milestones I want to reach, such as buying a home, starting a business, or retiring comfortably?
c) How do I envision my ideal financial future?
d) By defining your financial goals, you create a roadmap for your financial journey. These goals can be both tangible

(like saving a certain amount of money) and intangible (like achieving peace of mind regarding your finances).

Assessing Your Current Financial Situation

To build a strong financial foundation, you need to know where you stand today. This involves a comprehensive assessment of your current financial situation. Here's what you should look into:

- **Income:** Calculate your total income, including your salary, any side hustle earnings, rental income, or investments.
- **Expenses:** Create a detailed list of your monthly expenses. This should cover necessities like housing, food, transportation, as well as discretionary spending like entertainment.
- **Debts:** Make a list of all your outstanding debts, including credit card balances, loans, and mortgages. Note their interest rates and monthly payments.
- **Savings:** Determine how much you have saved in various accounts, such as your emergency fund, retirement savings, and other investments.

This assessment is like taking a snapshot of your financial life. It allows you to see where your money is coming from and where it's going. It's a crucial step in developing a financial plan that aligns with your goals.

The Psychological Aspects of Money Management and Mindset Shifts

Money management isn't just about numbers; it's deeply intertwined with your psychology and mindset. Understanding these aspects is key to making lasting changes in your financial habits.

- **Mindset Shifts:** Often, our attitudes and beliefs about money can hinder financial success. Are you someone who believes that money is hard to come by, or do you have a growth mindset when it comes to your finances? Recognizing and working on shifting limiting beliefs can be transformative.

- **Emotional Spending:** Many of us make impulsive financial decisions driven by emotions. Identifying your emotional triggers and finding healthier ways to cope with them can help you avoid unnecessary spending.
- **Delayed Gratification:** Cultivating the ability to delay gratification is essential for long-term financial success. It means choosing to save and invest for the future instead of splurging on immediate desires.
- **Financial Stress:** Money-related stress can take a toll on your mental and physical health. We'll explore strategies to manage and reduce financial stress, such as budgeting and building an emergency fund.

As we navigate through this first chapter, remember that building a strong foundation is the key to achieving financial success. By understanding your goals, evaluating your current financial situation, and addressing the psychological aspects of money, you'll be well-prepared to embark on the rest of your budgeting journey. Each step you take is a step toward greater financial empowerment and control.

CHAPTER 2: THE BASICS OF BUDGETING

At its core, budgeting is the art of assigning a purpose to every dollar that flows into your life. In this chapter, we'll delve into the fundamental concepts that underpin effective budgeting. From understanding the essence of a budget to exploring various budgeting methods, you'll gain the knowledge needed to start shaping your financial journey with intention.

Imagine your finances as a puzzle, with income on one side and expenses on the other. A budget is the blueprint that brings this puzzle together, aligning your financial goals and aspirations with the reality of your income and spending. It serves as a financial roadmap, helping you make informed decisions about where your money goes. By creating a budget, you're not just tracking expenses; you're taking control of your financial destiny.

At its core, a budget is a financial plan that outlines your expected income and your planned expenses over a specific period, usually a month or a year. It's like a detailed map that guides your financial journey. Here's why a budget is crucial:

1. Financial Awareness: A budget provides a clear picture of your financial situation. It helps you see how much money you have coming in and where it's going out. This awareness is the first step toward managing your money effectively.

2. Goal Alignment: Your budget acts as a bridge between your financial goals and your current financial situation. It ensures that your spending aligns with your aspirations. Whether you want to save for a home, pay off debt, or invest for retirement, a budget helps you allocate resources to achieve these goals.

3. Informed Decision-Making: With a budget, you make financial decisions based on data rather than impulse. It empowers you to prioritize spending and make informed choices about where your money should be allocated.

4. Financial Control: Creating a budget gives you a sense of control over your finances. It allows you to set limits on various spending categories and avoid overspending. This control can reduce financial stress and anxiety.

In essence, a budget is a tool that brings clarity and structure to your financial life. It enables you to take control of your income and expenses, ultimately leading to better financial health and the achievement of your financial goals. In the following sections of this chapter, we will explore various budgeting methods and provide guidance on setting realistic and achievable financial goals, all of which are essential components of effective budgeting.

Different Budgeting Methods: Zero-Based, Envelope System, 50/30/20 Rule, etc.

No two individuals or families are the same, which is why there's no one-size-fits-all approach to budgeting. We'll introduce you to several popular budgeting methods, each catering to different preferences and financial situations.

1. Zero-Based Budgeting: Zero-based budgeting is a meticulous approach to budgeting that ensures every dollar you earn has a designated purpose. In other words, your income minus your expenses should equal zero. Here's how it works:

You start by listing all your sources of income for a specific period, such as a month.

Then, you create categories for all your expenses, including fixed bills like rent or mortgage, groceries, transportation, entertainment, and savings.

For each category, you allocate a specific amount of money. The goal is to allocate your entire income, so there's no money left unaccounted for.

Throughout the month, you track your spending to ensure it aligns with your allocated amounts.

Zero-based budgeting encourages meticulous tracking of your finances and helps you prioritize your spending based on your financial goals. It's a method that leaves no room for unallocated funds.

2. Envelope System: The envelope system is a tangible and hands-on approach to budgeting, ideal for those who prefer to use cash for certain expenses. Here's how it works:

You create physical envelopes for different spending categories, such as groceries, entertainment, dining out, and more.

At the beginning of each budgeting period, you withdraw cash from your bank account and distribute it into these envelopes according to your budgeted amounts.

When you need to make a purchase in a specific category, you use the cash from the corresponding envelope.

Once the cash in an envelope is gone, you can't spend more in that category until the next budgeting period.

The envelope system encourages mindful spending because it makes you physically handle money for each expense. When the cash is gone from an envelope, it serves as a clear signal to stop spending in that category. It's a great method for those looking to curb discretionary spending.

3. 50/30/20 Rule: The 50/30/20 rule is a simplified budgeting method that divides your income into three main categories:

Needs (50%): This category includes essential expenses like rent or mortgage, utilities, groceries, transportation, and insurance. These are the expenses you can't do without.

Wants (30%): This category covers discretionary spending, such as dining out, entertainment, shopping, and other non-essential expenses.

Savings (20%): This portion of your income is dedicated to savings and debt repayment. It includes contributions to your emergency fund, retirement accounts, and paying down debts.

The 50/30/20 rule offers simplicity and flexibility. It's a great starting point for those new to budgeting and provides a clear guideline for how to allocate your income.

These budgeting methods provide you with options to tailor your budget to your unique style and financial goals. The key is to choose the method that best aligns with your financial situation and preferences. Remember that the goal of any budget is to help you manage your money effectively and work toward your financial aspirations.

Setting Realistic and Achievable Budgeting Goals

Goals provide direction and purpose to your budgeting efforts. In this section, we'll help you establish clear and achievable financial objectives. Whether you're aiming to pay off debt, build an emergency fund, or save for a dream vacation, setting the right goals is essential for a successful budget.

We'll guide you through the SMART (Specific, Measurable, Achievable, Relevant, Time-bound) criteria to ensure your goals are well-defined and within reach. Furthermore, we'll discuss the importance of breaking down larger goals into smaller, manageable milestones, making your budgeting journey more satisfying and attainable.

1. SMART Criteria: To ensure your goals are well-defined and attainable, use the SMART criteria:

- **Specific:** Clearly define your goals. Instead of a vague goal like "saving money," be specific. For example, "saving $5,000 for a down payment on a home" is much clearer.
- **Measurable:** Make your goals quantifiable. You should be able to track your progress. For instance, "paying off $10,000 in student loans" allows you to measure your success.
- **Achievable:** Ensure your goals are realistic given your current financial situation. Setting unattainable goals can lead to frustration. It's okay to aim high, but also consider whether the goal is feasible.
- **Relevant:** Your goals should align with your values and aspirations. They should be meaningful to you. If you're not passionate about your goal, it's harder to stay committed.
- **Time-bound:** Set a timeframe for achieving your goals. This creates a sense of urgency and helps you stay on track. For instance, "saving $2,000 for a summer vacation in 12 months" provides a clear deadline.

2. Break Down Larger Goals: Large financial goals can be overwhelming. To make them more manageable and less daunting, break them down into smaller, achievable milestones. For example, if your long-term goal is to save $10,000 for a down payment on a house, break it into smaller monthly or quarterly savings targets.

3. Prioritize Your Goals: Not all goals are equally important. Identify which goals are your top priorities. Focus your budgeting efforts on these key objectives while allocating a smaller portion of your income to less pressing goals. This ensures you're directing your resources where they're needed most.

4. Review and Adjust: Regularly review your goals and your progress. Life circumstances can change, and your financial goals may need adjustment accordingly. Be flexible and willing to adapt your budget as needed.

5. Celebrate Milestones: When you achieve a smaller milestone or reach one of your goals, celebrate your success. It's essential to acknowledge your achievements along the way, as this can boost your motivation and keep you on track.

As you immerse yourself in the basics of budgeting, remember that this chapter lays the groundwork for the strategies you'll employ to manage your money effectively. By understanding the purpose of a budget, exploring different methods, and setting realistic goals, you're equipping yourself with the tools to bring your financial aspirations to life. Each budget you create is a step closer to a more secure and empowered financial future.

CHAPTER 3: TRACKING INCOME AND EXPENSES

Just as a ship's captain relies on navigational tools to chart a course, your budget requires accurate data to steer your financial journey. In this chapter, we'll dive deep into the art of tracking your income and expenses. By understanding where your money comes from and where it goes, you'll gain unprecedented control over your financial decisions.

Identifying All Sources of Income

Income isn't limited to your primary job or salary; it encompasses all the way money flows into your life. Understanding and cataloging every source of income is a fundamental step in effective budgeting. Here's why it's crucial:

1. Comprehensive Financial Picture: By identifying all sources of income, you create a comprehensive financial picture. This includes not only your primary job but also any secondary sources of income.

2. Informed Decision-Making: A complete understanding of your income allows for informed decision-making in your budget. It helps you allocate your resources strategically based on all available funds.

3. Uncovering Opportunities: Sometimes, we have additional income sources we may not fully utilize or even realize.

Identifying these sources can reveal opportunities for saving, investing, or paying off debt more efficiently.

Now, let's explore some common sources of income to consider when creating your budget:

i. **Primary Job Salary:** This is typically your main source of income, the money you earn from your full-time or part-time job.

ii. **Side Gigs:** If you have a side hustle or freelance work, the income from these activities should be included in your budget.

iii. **Rental Income:** If you own property and receive rental income, it's an essential part of your financial inflow.

iv. **Investments:** Income from investments, such as dividends from stocks, interest from savings accounts, or rental income from real estate investments, should be included.

v. **Bonuses and Commissions:** If you receive periodic bonuses or commissions in addition to your regular salary, account for these as well.

vi. **Social Security or Retirement Benefits:** If you're eligible for Social Security benefits or receive retirement income, be sure to include them in your budget.

vii. **Other Sources:** Any other sources of income, such as child support, alimony, or royalties, should also be considered.

To create an accurate and effective budget, gather documentation from these income sources, such as pay stubs, bank statements, or tax documents. This information will provide a clear understanding of the total funds available for managing your finances.

Once you've identified and cataloged all sources of income, you can move forward with creating a budget that considers your complete financial inflow. This comprehensive approach will enable you to make informed decisions, set realistic goals, and ensure that your budget reflects your true financial situation.

Categorizing Expenses: Fixed, Variable, Discretionary, and Non-Discretionary

Expenses come in various forms, and understanding their categories is essential for effective budgeting. Categorizing expenses helps you gain insight into your spending patterns, make informed financial decisions, and identify areas where you can save. Here are the key expense categories to consider:

1. Fixed Expenses: Fixed expenses are costs that remain consistent each month. They are typically obligations that you must pay regularly and are often essential. Examples include:

- Rent or Mortgage Payments
- Loan Payments (Car loans, student loans, etc.)
- Insurance Premiums (Health, auto, home, etc.)
- Membership Fees (Gym, subscriptions, etc.)
- Property Taxes

These expenses are predictable and essential for maintaining your basic lifestyle.

2. Variable Expenses: Variable expenses are costs that can fluctuate from month to month. They are less predictable than fixed expenses but are still necessary for daily living. Examples include:

- Groceries
- Utilities (Electricity, water, gas, etc.)
- Transportation (Fuel, public transit, maintenance)
- Medical Expenses (Prescriptions, doctor's visits)

- Clothing
- Entertainment (Movies, dining out, hobbies)

Variable expenses can vary based on your choices and lifestyle. Monitoring them can help you identify opportunities for savings.

3. Discretionary Expenses: Discretionary expenses encompass non-essential spending. These are the costs associated with activities and purchases that enhance your quality of life but are not absolute necessities. Examples include:

- Dining Out
- Entertainment (Concerts, movies, vacations)
- Hobbies (Golf, gaming, crafting)
- Shopping (Clothing, electronics, home decor)

Discretionary expenses are often the easiest to cut back on when you need to tighten your budget or redirect funds towards savings goals.

4. Non-Discretionary Expenses: Non-discretionary expenses are necessities that are vital for your basic well-being and survival. These are expenses that you can't easily cut or eliminate without impacting your quality of life. Examples include:

- Groceries
- Rent or Mortgage
- Utilities
- Transportation for work or medical needs
- Health Insurance

These expenses are the core of your budget and should be prioritized when allocating your income.

When creating a budget, it's crucial to categorize your expenses accurately. Start by listing all your monthly expenses and assigning them to the appropriate categories. This process provides a clear view of your financial commitments and discretionary spending. It also allows you to identify areas where you can adjust achieve your financial goals, whether that's saving for a vacation, paying off debt, or building an emergency fund.

By categorizing your expenses, you gain control over your financial decisions and can make informed choices that align with your budgeting priorities.

Gone are the days of manual record-keeping in notebooks. Budgeting tools and apps have revolutionized the way we manage our finances. These digital solutions offer several benefits:

a) **Automation:** Many expense tracking apps can automatically sync with your bank and credit card accounts, saving you the hassle of manual data entry.

b) **Real-Time Updates:** With digital tools, you can see your financial data in real-time. This allows for better decision-making as you always have an up-to-date view of your financial situation.

c) **Categorization:** Most apps categorize your expenses automatically, helping you understand where your money is going. You can also customize categories to suit your needs.

d) **Insights and Reports:** These tools often provide detailed reports and visual representations of your spending patterns. This can be invaluable for identifying areas where you can cut back or optimize your budget.

e) **Accessibility:** You can access your financial data from anywhere with an internet connection, making it convenient for tracking expenses on the go.

Here are some popular types of expense tracking tools and apps:

1. Budgeting Apps:

i. **Mint:** A comprehensive budgeting app that

automatically categorizes expenses and provides a complete financial overview.

ii. **YNAB (You Need a Budget):** Focuses on allocating your income to specific categories, encouraging you to budget your dollars.

iii. **Personal Capital:** Combines budgeting and investment tracking, making it suitable for those with diverse financial portfolios.

2. Expense Tracking Apps:

i. **Expensify:** Designed for business expense tracking but can be used for personal finances as well.

ii. **Receipts by Wave:** Allows you to capture and organize receipts for easy expense tracking.

3. Banking Apps:

i. Many banks offer mobile apps with built-in expense tracking features that automatically categorize your spending.

4. Spreadsheet Software:

i. If you prefer a more hands-on approach, spreadsheet software like Microsoft Excel or Google Sheets can be customized to create your expense tracking system.

When choosing an expense tracking tool or app, consider your preferences and needs. Some people prefer the simplicity and mobility of mobile apps, while others may want the customization options of spreadsheets. The key is to find a tool that fits your style and helps you stay on top of your finances.

As you embark on your expense tracking journey, remember that the knowledge gained from this process forms the foundation for building a budget that aligns with your financial goals and aspirations. By harnessing the power of these digital tools, you'll be well-equipped to make informed financial decisions and achieve your financial objectives.

CHAPTER 4: CREATING YOUR BUDGET

Now that you've gathered the necessary tools and insights, it's time to put them to work. In this chapter, we'll guide you through the process of crafting a budget that reflects your financial aspirations, helping you allocate your resources wisely and strategically.

Designing a Budget that Aligns with Your Financial Goals

Your budget isn't just a list of numbers; it's a powerful tool that reflects your values, priorities, and long-term ambitions. Creating a budget that resonates with your financial goals is like designing a roadmap to guide you toward your desired financial destinations. Whether you're working toward paying off debt, saving for a down payment on a house, or planning a dream vacation, here's how to craft a budget that aligns with your objectives:

- **Clearly Define Your Financial Goals:** Begin by setting specific, measurable, achievable, relevant, and time-bound (SMART) financial goals. Whether it's eliminating high-interest debt, building an emergency fund, or saving for retirement, having clear objectives provides purpose and direction for your budget.
- **Prioritize Your Goals:** Not all financial goals have the same urgency. Identify your top priorities and allocate a larger

portion of your budget to these objectives. For example, if paying off credit card debt is your primary goal, allocate more funds to debt repayment.

- **Create Categories and Allocate Funds:** Break down your budget into categories that align with your spending habits and financial goals. Common categories include housing, transportation, groceries, debt repayment, savings, and discretionary spending. Allocate specific amounts to each category based on your financial goals and available income.
- **Monitor and Adjust:** Consistently track your spending to ensure it aligns with your budget. Utilize expense tracking tools or apps to help with this process. If you notice that you're overspending in one category, adjust your budget accordingly by reducing spending in another area.
- **Review and Reflect:** Periodically review your budget to assess your progress toward your financial goals. Celebrate your achievements, no matter how small, and adjust as needed. Life circumstances can change, so your budget should be flexible to accommodate these changes.
- **Stay Committed and Stay on Course:** Designing a budget that aligns with your financial goals is just the first step. Staying committed to your budget and consistently following it is essential for success. Remember that achieving your financial goals may require discipline and sacrifices, but the long-term benefits are well worth it.
- **Seek Professional Guidance if Needed:** If you have complex financial goals or need assistance with specific aspects of your budget, consider consulting a financial advisor or counselor. They can provide expert guidance tailored to your unique situation.

Your budget is a dynamic tool that evolves with your financial journey. By aligning it with your values and ambitions, you're not just managing your money; you're taking deliberate steps toward the life you desire. As you make intentional decisions about your spending and saving, you'll be on the path to achieving your financial objectives and securing a more prosperous future.

Allocating Funds to Different Expense Categories

Think of your budget as a canvas on which you paint your financial future. This section will show you how to allocate your funds to different expense categories—each stroke of the brush representing a portion of your income. We'll revisit the categories we discussed earlier, such as fixed, variable, discretionary, and non-discretionary expenses. By breaking down your budget into these categories, you gain a comprehensive overview of where your money is going and can make informed adjustments as needed.

1. Fixed Expenses: Fixed expenses are the cornerstone of your budget. These are the recurring, predictable costs that remain consistent each month. To allocate funds to fixed expenses:

- List all your fixed expenses, including rent or mortgage payments, loan payments, insurance premiums, and membership fees.
- Dedicate a portion of your income to cover these expenses. Ensure that the allocated amount fully covers your fixed obligations.

2. Variable Expenses: Variable expenses are the flexible costs that can fluctuate from month to month. To allocate funds to variable expenses:

- Identify your variable expenses, such as groceries, utilities, transportation, medical expenses, and clothing.
- Allocate an estimated amount to each variable expense category based on your historical spending patterns and needs. Be prepared for some variability in these categories.

3. Discretionary Expenses: Discretionary expenses encompass non-essential spending that enhances your lifestyle but isn't strictly necessary. To allocate funds to discretionary expenses:

- Categorize your discretionary expenses, including dining out, entertainment, hobbies, and shopping.
- Allocate a portion of your income to these categories. Keep in mind that discretionary spending should align with your financial goals and priorities. Consider trimming this category if necessary to allocate more to savings or debt repayment.

4. Non-Discretionary Expenses: Non-discretionary expenses are vital for your basic well-being and survival. To allocate funds to non-discretionary expenses:

- Prioritize non-discretionary expenses like groceries, rent or mortgage, utilities, transportation for work or medical needs, and health insurance.
- Allocate enough to cover these necessities. Ensure that these expenses are fully funded before allocating funds to discretionary spending.

5. Savings and Goals: Don't forget to allocate funds for savings and financial goals. This includes contributions to your emergency fund, retirement savings, debt repayment, and specific savings goals like a vacation or a down payment on a house.

- Set aside a portion of your income for savings and goals. Make this allocation a priority to ensure that you're actively working toward your financial aspirations.

6. Regularly Review and Adjust: Your budget is not set in stone. Regularly review your income and expenses, and adjust your allocations as needed. Life circumstances change, and your budget should be flexible to accommodate those changes.

By allocating funds to different expense categories, you create a financial framework that aligns with your income and aspirations. This process provides a clear overview of where your money is going, enabling you to make informed adjustments and prioritize your financial goals. Remember that your budget is a dynamic tool that evolves with your financial journey, so stay proactive and committed to your financial plan.

Incorporating Savings and Emergency Funds into Your Budget

Saving money is one of the most important aspects of budgeting. We'll explore how to allocate funds for savings goals, such as building an emergency fund, creating a vacation fund, or contributing to retirement accounts. An emergency fund is your financial safety net, providing peace of mind in times of unexpected expenses. We'll guide you through setting up and maintaining an emergency fund that's tailored to your needs. By making saving a priority in your budget, you're ensuring that you're prepared for whatever life may throw your way.

Here's how to incorporate savings into your budget:

1. Emergency Fund: An emergency fund is a financial cushion that provides peace of mind in times of unexpected expenses or emergencies, such as medical bills, car repairs, or job loss. Here's how to allocate funds for your emergency fund:

- **Determine Your Emergency Fund Goal:** Start by setting a specific savings goal for your emergency fund. Financial experts often recommend saving at least three to six months' worth of living expenses. Customize this amount based on your individual circumstances and comfort level.
- **Create a Dedicated Category:** In your budget, create a separate category for your emergency fund. Allocate a portion of your income each month to this category until you reach your savings goal.
- **Prioritize Consistency:** Consistency is key when building an emergency fund. Treat your savings for emergencies as a non-negotiable expense, just like rent or utilities. This

ensures that you're steadily working toward your goal.

- **Automate Savings:** Consider setting up an automatic transfer from your checking account to your dedicated emergency fund savings account. This "pay yourself first" approach ensures that you save before spending.
- **Use Windfalls Wisely:** When you receive unexpected windfalls like tax refunds, bonuses, or gifts, consider allocating a portion to your emergency fund to boost your savings progress.

2. Other Savings Goals: Beyond your emergency fund, you may have other savings goals, such as a vacation fund, retirement savings, or saving for a down payment on a house. Here's how to incorporate these into your budget:

- **Prioritize Goals:** Identify your savings goals and prioritize them based on urgency and importance. Allocate a portion of your income to each goal category.
- **Set Specific Targets:** Define specific savings targets for each goal, such as saving a certain amount for your next vacation or contributing a specific percentage of your income to your retirement accounts.
- **Regularly Review and Adjust:** Periodically review your progress toward your savings goals and make adjustments as needed. If you receive a salary increase or experience changes in expenses, consider reallocating funds to accelerate your savings.

By incorporating savings and emergency funds into your budget, you're proactively preparing for future financial challenges and opportunities. Remember that your budget is a dynamic tool that adapts to your changing circumstances. It empowers you to make informed decisions, prioritize your financial goals, and build a solid financial foundation. Ultimately, budgeting and saving are powerful steps toward achieving financial success and resilience.

CHAPTER 5: MANAGING DEBT

Debt can cast a shadow over even the most promising financial prospects, but it's not an insurmountable challenge. In this chapter, we'll delve into effective strategies for managing your existing debts, preventing further debt accumulation, and integrating debt management into your budgeting journey.

Strategies for Dealing with Existing Debts

The weight of debt can feel overwhelming, but with a clear plan, you can conquer it. We'll discuss various strategies for managing existing debts, from credit card balances to student loans. We'll explore methods like the debt snowball and the debt avalanche, both designed to help you make progress in paying off your debts strategically. By prioritizing payments and staying focused, you can chip away at your debts one step at a time.

Let's explore some effective strategies for managing and paying off different types of debts:

1. Create a Comprehensive List: Begin by making a list of all your existing debts. Include details such as the type of debt (e.g., credit card, student loan, personal loan), the outstanding balance, interest rates, minimum monthly payments, and the due dates. Having a clear overview of your debts is the first step toward managing them effectively.

2. Prioritize Your Debts: Not all debts are created equal. To prioritize your debts, consider the following factors:

- **Interest Rates:** Start by tackling high-interest debts first, as they cost you more in the long run. This is known as the debt avalanche method.
- **Minimum Payments:** Ensure that you make at least the minimum monthly payments on all your debts to avoid penalties and late fees.
- **Emotional Satisfaction:** Alternatively, you can use the debt snowball method, where you focus on paying off the smallest debt first. This approach provides emotional satisfaction as you eliminate individual debts quickly, which can boost your motivation.

3. Create a Budget: Design a detailed budget that considers all your income and expenses, including your debt payments. Allocate a portion of your income specifically for debt repayment.

4. Cut Non-Essential Expenses: Identify areas where you can cut discretionary spending to free up more money for debt repayment. This may involve reducing dining out, entertainment expenses, or subscription services temporarily.

5. Negotiate Lower Interest Rates: Contact your creditors and inquire about the possibility of lowering your interest rates. A good payment history and a polite request can sometimes result in reduced rates, which can save you money over time.

6. Consider Debt Consolidation: Debt consolidation involves combining multiple debts into a single, lower-interest loan. This can simplify your debt management and reduce your overall interest costs. Be cautious and ensure that the terms of the consolidation loan are favorable before proceeding.

7. Create a Debt Repayment Plan: Choose a debt repayment strategy that aligns with your goals and financial situation. Whether you opt for the debt avalanche, debt snowball, or a hybrid approach, having a clear plan with specific goals will keep you on track.

8. Stay Committed: Paying off debts requires discipline and perseverance. Stick to your budget and repayment plan consistently. Celebrate each milestone and keep your long-term financial goals in mind as motivation.

9. Seek Professional Help if Needed: If you're struggling to manage your debts, consider seeking assistance from a credit counselor or a debt management agency. They can provide guidance, negotiate with creditors on your behalf, and help you create a manageable repayment plan.

Remember that becoming debt-free is a journey that takes time and effort. Stay patient and focused, and gradually, you'll make progress in paying off your debts. Each payment brings you closer to financial freedom and a more secure financial future.

How to Avoid Accumulating More Debt

Prevention is key to maintaining a healthy financial life. We'll delve into the habits and practices that can help you avoid accumulating more debt in the future. From distinguishing between needs and wants to cultivating a mindful spending mindset, you'll learn how to make decisions that align with your financial goals and aspirations.

1. Distinguish Between Needs and Wants: One of the fundamental principles of responsible financial management is distinguishing between needs and wants. Needs are essential expenses necessary for your well-being, such as housing, food, utilities, and transportation. Wants are non-essential, discretionary expenses like dining out, entertainment, and luxury purchases.

- Prioritize your needs in your budget, ensuring they are fully covered before allocating funds to wants.

2. Create and Follow a Budget: A well-structured budget is your financial roadmap. It helps you allocate your income effectively, avoid overspending, and plan for your financial goals.

- Regularly review your budget to ensure that your spending aligns with your financial priorities.

3. Build an Emergency Fund: Having an emergency fund is a crucial safety net that can prevent you from accumulating debt when unexpected expenses arise.

- Aim to save at least three to six months' worth of living expenses in your emergency fund.

4. Pay Off Credit Card Balances Monthly: If you use credit cards, strive to pay off your balances in full each month. Carrying a balance on credit cards can lead to high-interest charges and debt accumulation.

5. Limit Credit Card Use: Use credit cards wisely and sparingly. Reserve them for necessary expenses and emergencies, rather than as a primary payment method for discretionary spending.

6. Avoid Impulse Purchases: Before making a purchase, especially a significant one, take time to evaluate whether it's a need or a want. Avoid impulse buying by implementing a waiting period before making non-essential purchases.

7. Set Savings Goals: Establish specific savings goals for various purposes, such as retirement, a vacation, or a down payment on a house.

- Allocate a portion of your income toward these goals each month.

8. Educate Yourself: Continuously educate yourself about personal finance and money management. Knowledge is a powerful tool for making informed financial decisions.

9. Cultivate a Mindful Spending Mindset: Practice mindful spending by questioning whether a purchase aligns with your long-term financial goals.

- Ask yourself if a purchase will truly enhance your life and if it's worth the financial trade-off.

10. Review Your Financial Goals Regularly: Periodically revisit your financial goals to stay motivated and focused on your long-term objectives.

11. Seek Professional Advice if Necessary: If you're facing financial challenges or struggling to manage your debts, consider seeking guidance from a financial counselor or advisor. They can provide tailored advice and strategies to help you stay on track.

By adopting these habits and practices, you can cultivate a mindful and responsible approach to your finances. Preventing the accumulation of more debt is not only about managing your money but also about making conscious decisions that align with your financial aspirations and long-term well-being.

Incorporating Debt Payments into Your Budget

Debt repayment is an essential part of your financial journey, and it needs a place in your budget. We'll guide you through the process of incorporating debt payments into your budget, ensuring that you allocate funds specifically for this purpose. By making debt payments a non-negotiable item in your budget, you're taking an active step toward your financial freedom. We'll show you how to strike a balance between debt repayment and other financial goals, ensuring that your overall budget remains realistic and achievable.

1. Assess Your Debt Obligations: Start by listing all your existing debts, including credit card balances, student loans, personal loans, and any other outstanding loans. Gather information on the outstanding balances, interest rates, minimum monthly payments, and due dates for each debt.

2. Prioritize Your Debts: Determine which debts to prioritize based on factors like interest rates, outstanding balances, and any high-priority debts that need immediate attention. High-interest debts should typically take precedence.

3. Set a Debt Repayment Goal: Define your debt repayment goal. How quickly do you want to pay off your debts? Setting a specific timeline can provide motivation and direction.

4. Create a Debt Payment Category: In your budget, establish a dedicated category for debt payments. This category should include all your minimum monthly payments plus any extra funds you can allocate toward debt repayment.

5. Allocate Funds Wisely: Allocate a portion of your monthly income to your debt payment category. Ensure that you allocate enough to cover all your minimum payments while making progress on high-priority debts.

6. Trim Discretionary Spending: Identify areas in your budget where you can reduce discretionary spending, such as dining out, entertainment, or non-essential subscriptions. Redirect these funds toward your debt repayment category.

7. Make Extra Payments: If possible, make extra payments toward high-interest debts to accelerate your progress. Even small additional payments can significantly reduce the time it takes to pay off a debt.

8. Automate Payments: Consider automating your minimum monthly payments to ensure you never miss a due date. Timely payments help maintain a good credit history.

9. Track Your Progress: Regularly monitor your debt repayment progress. Celebrate milestones as you pay off individual debts or reach specific goals.

10. Review and Adjust: Periodically review your budget to assess your debt repayment strategy. As your financial situation changes, you may need to adjust your allocation of funds to debt payments.

11. Balance Debt Repayment with Other Goals: While debt repayment is essential, it's also crucial to strike a balance with other financial goals. Allocate funds to savings, emergency funds, and other priorities to ensure a well-rounded financial plan.

12. Seek Professional Help if Needed: If you're struggling to manage your debt or create a sustainable budget, consider seeking guidance from a financial counselor or advisor. They can provide personalized strategies and support.

Incorporating debt payments into your budget makes them a non-negotiable part of your financial plan. This approach ensures that you stay on track with your debt repayment goals and gradually work toward financial freedom. With discipline, commitment, and a well-structured budget, you can make meaningful progress in paying off your debts and building a secure financial future.

As you navigate the realm of debt management, remember that this chapter empowers you to take control of your financial destiny. By implementing strategies to tackle existing debts, preventing new debts from accumulating, and weaving debt payments into your budget, you're breaking the cycle of financial stress and moving closer to your desired state of financial well-being.

CHAPTER 6: SAVING AND INVESTING

Saving and investing are the cornerstones of building a secure financial future. In this chapter, we'll explore the significance of saving for both short-term needs and long-term aspirations. We'll also delve into the world of investing, equipping you with essential knowledge to make informed decisions about growing your wealth.

The Importance of Saving for Short-Term and Long-Term Goals

Saving is more than just setting aside money—it's a strategy that empowers you to meet your financial objectives. We'll discuss the importance of building an emergency fund to handle unexpected expenses. This safety net provides peace of mind and financial security. Additionally, we'll explore how to save for short-term goals like a vacation or a major purchase, as well as long-term goals like retirement or buying a home.

Let's delve into the importance of saving for various objectives:

1. Building an Emergency Fund:

Importance: An emergency fund is your financial safety net. It provides peace of mind and financial security by covering unexpected expenses like medical bills, car repairs, or job loss without resorting to high-interest debt.

How to Save: Allocate a portion of your income specifically for your emergency fund. Start by saving at least three to six months' worth of living expenses. Gradually increase this amount to provide even greater financial stability.

2. Saving for Short-Term Goals:

Importance: Saving for short-term goals, such as a vacation, a new car, or a major purchase, allows you to enjoy life's pleasures without relying on credit or depleting your emergency fund.

How to Save:

- **Set Specific Goals:** Define your short-term goals with clear targets and timelines. Knowing what you're saving for provides motivation.
- **Create a Dedicated Savings Account:** Open a separate savings account for each short-term goal. This makes it easy to track your progress.
- **Automate Savings:** Set up automatic transfers from your checking account to your short-term savings accounts to ensure consistent contributions.
- **Budget Wisely:** Adjust your budget to allocate funds to these savings goals. Consider cutting discretionary spending to accelerate your savings.

3. Saving for Long-Term Goals:

Importance: Long-term goals like retirement, buying a home, or funding a child's education require substantial savings over an extended period. Starting early maximizes your ability to achieve these goals.

How to Save:

- **Prioritize Retirement:** Start saving for retirement as

early as possible. Contribute to retirement accounts like a 401(k) or an IRA. Take advantage of employer matching contributions if available.

- **Invest Wisely:** Consider investing your long-term savings in diversified investment vehicles to potentially achieve higher returns over time.
- **Set Clear Targets:** Define specific financial targets for long-term goals, whether it's a down payment for a home or a certain amount for retirement.
- **Regularly Review and Adjust:** Periodically review your progress toward long-term goals and adjust your savings strategy as needed.
- **Seek Professional Guidance:** Consult with a financial advisor to create a personalized plan for achieving your long-term financial goals.

By aligning your savings with your goals, you transform your aspirations into actionable plans. This not only helps you achieve what you desire in life but also provides financial security and peace of mind. Saving is a powerful tool that empowers you to manage your finances proactively and build a solid foundation for your financial future.

Understanding Different Types of Savings Accounts

Not all savings accounts are created equal. We'll dive into the world of savings accounts, from traditional savings accounts offered by banks to high-yield online savings accounts. We'll explore the features, benefits, and limitations of each type, helping you choose an account that best suits your needs.

Common types of savings accounts:

1. Traditional Savings Accounts:

Features:

- Typically offered by brick-and-mortar banks.
- Low or minimal fees.
- Lower interest rates compared to other types of accounts.
- Easy access to funds via ATMs, branches, and online banking.
- Often linked to your checking account for easy transfers.

Benefits:

- Convenience and accessibility.
- Provides a safe place to save money.

Limitations:

- Lower interest rates mean your money may not grow as quickly.
- Minimal returns may not keep pace with inflation.

2. High-Yield Savings Accounts:

Features:

- Offered by online banks or credit unions.
- Competitive interest rates, often higher than traditional savings accounts.
- May have no or low fees.
- Typically accessed online or through mobile apps.
- Limited or no physical branch access.

Benefits:

- Higher interest rates mean your money can grow faster.
- Easy access to funds online.
- No or low fees can help you maximize savings.

Limitations:

- Limited or no in-person banking services.
- May require a minimum balance to earn the advertised

interest rate.

3. Money Market Accounts (MMAs):

Features:

- Offered by banks and credit unions.
- Higher interest rates compared to traditional savings accounts.
- May come with limited check-writing capabilities.
- May require a higher minimum balance.

Benefits:

- Competitive interest rates.
- A degree of liquidity through check-writing.
- Generally lower fees than some other accounts.

Limitations:

- Some MMAs require a higher minimum balance.
- Limited check-writing capabilities compared to a checking account.

4. Certificate of Deposit (CD):

Features:

- Offered by banks and credit unions.
- Fixed-term savings with higher interest rates than regular savings accounts.
- Penalties for early withdrawal before the CD's maturity date.
- Terms can range from a few months to several years.

Benefits:

- Higher interest rates than traditional savings accounts.
- Money is locked in for a fixed period, promoting long-term savings.

Limitations:

- Limited access to funds until the CD matures.
- Penalties for early withdrawal.

5. Roth Individual Retirement Account (Roth IRA):

Features:

- Retirement savings account with potential tax advantages.
- Contributions are made with after-tax dollars.
- Earnings can grow tax-free, and qualified withdrawals are tax-free.

Benefits:

- Tax-free growth and withdrawals in retirement.
- Diverse investment options.
- May offer penalty-free early withdrawals for certain purposes like first-time homebuying or education.

Limitations:

- Contributions are subject to income limits.
- Not designed for short-term savings or emergency funds.

Choosing the right savings account depends on your financial goals and needs. For an emergency fund or short-term goals, a high-yield savings account or money market account may be suitable. If you're saving for retirement, a Roth IRA offers tax advantages. Certificates of deposit can be useful for longer-term savings, but they require you to lock in your funds for a specific period. Consider your liquidity needs, risk tolerance, and savings timeline when selecting the best savings account for your situation.

Introduction to Basic Investing Principles

Investing can be a powerful tool for growing your wealth, but it also comes with its own set of considerations. We'll introduce basic investing principles, demystifying concepts like stocks, bonds, mutual funds, and index funds. You'll learn how risk and reward play a role in investment decisions and how to assess your risk tolerance.

Fundamental concepts and principles:

1. Asset Classes:

- **Stocks:** Stocks represent ownership in a company. When you buy a stock, you own a portion of that company. Stocks offer the potential for high returns but come with higher volatility and risk.
- **Bonds:** Bonds are debt securities issued by governments, municipalities, or corporations. When you buy a bond, you're essentially lending money to the issuer in exchange for periodic interest payments and the return of the bond's face value at maturity. Bonds are generally considered less risky than stocks but may offer lower returns.

2. Mutual Funds: Mutual funds pool money from multiple investors to invest in a diversified portfolio of stocks, bonds, or other securities. They offer diversification and professional management but may come with fees.

3. Index Funds: Index funds are a type of mutual fund that aims to replicate the performance of a specific market index, such as the S&P 500. They tend to have lower fees than actively managed funds and provide broad market exposure.

4. Risk and Reward: Risk and reward are closely related in investing. Generally, investments with higher potential returns, like stocks, come with higher risk. Lower-risk investments, such as bonds, tend to offer lower returns. Your risk tolerance, which is your willingness and ability to withstand investment fluctuations, plays a crucial role in shaping your investment strategy.

5. Diversification: Diversification involves spreading your investments across different asset classes, industries, and regions. Diversified portfolios can help reduce risk because losses in one investment may be offset by gains in another.

6. Time Horizon: Your time horizon is the length of time you plan to hold your investments before needing access to the money. It greatly influences your investment choices. Longer time horizons may allow you to take on more risk, as you have more time to weather market fluctuations.

7. Dollar-Cost Averaging: Dollar-cost averaging is an investment strategy where you invest a fixed amount of money at regular intervals, regardless of market conditions. This approach can help reduce the impact of market volatility and is often used for long-term investing.

8. Risk Assessment: Assess your risk tolerance honestly. Consider factors like your investment goals, financial stability, and emotional comfort with market fluctuations. Your risk tolerance should align with your investment strategy.

9. Investment Goals: Define clear investment goals, such as saving for retirement, buying a home, or funding education. Your goals will influence your investment choices and time horizon.

10. Professional Advice: Consider seeking advice from a financial advisor or investment professional to create a personalized investment strategy that aligns with your goals and risk tolerance.

By gaining a foundational understanding of these basic investing principles, you'll be better equipped to make informed investment decisions that help you grow your wealth and work toward your financial goals. Remember that investing involves risk, and it's essential to have a well-thought-out strategy tailored to your unique financial situation.

As you delve into the world of saving and investing, remember that this chapter is about building a solid financial foundation. By prioritizing saving for both short-term and long-term goals, understanding the nuances of different savings accounts, and gaining insight into basic investing principles, you're positioning yourself for financial growth and security. Your savings and investment efforts are the seeds you plant today for the prosperous future you envision.

CHAPTER 7: NAVIGATING LIFE CHANGES

Life is full of twists and turns, and your budget should be flexible enough to adapt to these changes. In this chapter, we'll explore how to navigate major life events while maintaining financial stability. We'll also discuss strategies for managing unexpected setbacks and expenses, ensuring that your budget remains resilient in the face of uncertainty.

Adapting Your Budget to Major Life Events

Major life events like marriage, starting a family, or buying a house bring both joy and financial adjustments. We'll guide you through the process of adapting your budget to accommodate these changes. Whether you're combining finances with a partner, factoring in childcare expenses, or taking on a mortgage, your budget should reflect your new reality. We'll provide practical tips for reevaluating your income, expenses, and savings goals to ensure that your budget remains aligned with your aspirations.

Here's how you can adjust your budget for some common major life events:

1. Marriage:

- **Combine Finances:** If you're merging finances with a spouse, have open and honest discussions about your financial goals and priorities. Create a joint budget that reflects your shared financial responsibilities and aspirations.

- **Update Beneficiaries:** Review your insurance policies, retirement accounts, and wills to ensure they reflect your new marital status and beneficiaries.

2. Starting a Family:

- **Childcare Expenses:** Account for childcare expenses, including daycare or a nanny, in your budget. These can be significant costs that need to be planned for in advance.
- **Healthcare Costs:** Evaluate your health insurance coverage to ensure it meets your family's needs, especially if you're adding dependents to your plan.
- **Emergency Fund:** Consider increasing your emergency fund to cover unexpected family-related expenses.

3. Buying a House:

- **Mortgage Payments:** Incorporate your new mortgage payments, property taxes, and homeowner's insurance into your budget.
- **Maintenance Costs:** Budget for ongoing maintenance and repairs, which can vary based on the age and condition of your home.
- **Homeownership Expenses:** Don't forget about utilities, HOA fees (if applicable), and any new home-related costs.

4. Career Changes:

- **Salary Changes:** If you experience a significant salary increase or decrease due to a career change, adjust your budget accordingly. This may involve increasing your savings or reevaluating your spending habits.

5. Education Expenses:

- **College Tuition:** If you or your children are pursuing higher education, budget for tuition, books, and other educational expenses.

6. Retirement:

- **Increase Savings:** If you receive a windfall or experience a significant increase in income, consider increasing your retirement savings contributions to secure your future.

7. Unexpected Windfalls:

- **Plan Wisely:** If you receive an unexpected windfall, like an inheritance or a bonus, develop a plan for how you'll allocate these funds. Consider paying off debts, bolstering your emergency fund, and investing for the future.

8. Divorce or Separation:

- **Review Finances:** After a divorce or separation, conduct a thorough review of your finances. Update your budget to reflect your new income, expenses, and financial responsibilities.

9. Medical Expenses:

- **Healthcare Costs:** If you or a family member faces significant medical expenses, create a separate budget category for these costs to ensure they don't disrupt your overall financial plan.

10. Moving or Relocating:

- **Relocation Costs:** Budget for the expenses associated with moving, such as transportation, packing, and temporary lodging.

Remember that adapting your budget to major life events may

require some adjustments and flexibility. Regularly review and update your budget to ensure it remains aligned with your financial aspirations. Major life events can be opportunities to reevaluate your financial goals and make strategic decisions to secure your financial future.

Strategies for Managing Financial Setbacks and Unexpected Expenses

Financial setbacks are an inevitable part of life, but with a solid strategy, you can weather these storms without derailing your financial progress. We'll discuss the importance of an emergency fund as a safety net during times of unexpected expenses or job loss. Additionally, we'll explore strategies for managing medical emergencies, car repairs, or other unforeseen costs without jeopardizing your financial stability. By incorporating contingency plans into your budget, you're fostering resilience in the face of adversity.

Here are strategies to help you navigate these challenges:

1. Emergency Fund:

- **Importance:** An emergency fund is your first line of defense against financial setbacks. It provides a financial cushion to cover unexpected expenses or cope with job loss without resorting to debt.
- **How to Build and Use:** Aim to save at least three to six months' worth of living expenses in your emergency fund. Start small if necessary and gradually build it. Only use the fund for genuine emergencies, like medical bills, car repairs, or unexpected job loss.

2. Insurance:

- **Health Insurance:** Maintain adequate health insurance coverage to protect yourself and your family from high medical expenses.

- **Auto and Home Insurance:** Ensure your vehicles and property are adequately insured to cover repair or replacement costs in the event of accidents or damage.

3. Budget Contingency Fund:

- **Include in Your Budget:** Create a budget category for unexpected expenses or setbacks. Allocate a small portion of your income to this fund each month to build it over time.

4. Side Income or Gig Work:

- **Additional Sources of Income:** Explore opportunities for side gigs or freelance work to supplement your primary income. This extra income can help cover unexpected expenses.

5. Negotiation and Payment Plans:

- **Medical Bills:** If faced with high medical bills, negotiate with healthcare providers for reduced fees or set up manageable payment plans.
- **Debt Negotiation:** If you have outstanding debts, negotiate with creditors for more favorable repayment terms or settlements.

6. Prioritize and Cut Non-Essentials:

- **Assess Priorities:** When a financial setback occurs, evaluate your financial priorities. Temporarily cut non-essential expenses like dining out or entertainment to redirect funds toward immediate needs.

7. Financial Counseling:

- **Seek Professional Help:** If a financial setback feels overwhelming, consider consulting a financial counselor or advisor for guidance on managing the situation and creating a recovery plan.

8. Utilize Government Assistance:

- **Explore Options:** If eligible, research government assistance programs that can provide support during financial crises, such as unemployment benefits or food assistance.

9. Avoid High-Interest Debt:

- **Emergency Credit:** If you must use credit during a setback, try to avoid high-interest options like credit cards. Look for low-interest or 0% interest promotional offers if available.

10. Maintain a Long-Term Perspective:

- **Stay Committed to Goals:** Despite setbacks, maintain a long-term perspective on your financial goals. Continue saving for retirement and other long-term objectives as soon as your situation stabilizes.

Building an emergency fund, having the right insurance, and budgeting for contingencies are essential elements of a solid financial plan. Remember that setbacks are temporary, and your financial stability can be restored with careful planning and strategic decision-making.

As you navigate the complexities of life changes and unexpected setbacks, remember that this chapter equips you with the tools to maintain financial equilibrium. By adapting your budget to accommodate major life events and preparing for unexpected expenses, you're demonstrating your commitment to a stable and secure financial future. Your budget isn't static; it's a dynamic framework that evolves with you, supporting you through every twist and turn on your journey.

CHAPTER 8: STAYING DISCIPLINED AND MOTIVATED

Staying the course on your budgeting journey requires not only knowledge and planning but also a healthy dose of discipline and motivation. In this chapter, we'll delve into strategies for overcoming challenges, celebrating milestones, and maintaining the momentum that leads to lasting financial success.

Overcoming Budgeting Challenges and Setbacks

Budgeting isn't always smooth sailing. Unexpected expenses, lifestyle changes, or even moments of temptation can test your commitment to your financial goals. We'll discuss common budgeting challenges and provide practical solutions for staying on track. From managing splurges to reevaluating your budget after a setback, you'll learn how to navigate obstacles without derailing your progress.

1. Unexpected Expenses:

- **Challenge:** Unexpected bills or emergencies can disrupt your budget.
- **Solution:** Maintain an emergency fund to cover unexpected expenses. Revisit your budget periodically to adjust for these situations.

2. Lifestyle Changes:

- **Challenge:** Major life events like getting married, having children, or buying a house can impact your budget.

- **Solution:** Reevaluate your budget when lifestyle changes occur. Adjust your spending and savings goals to align with your new circumstances.

3. Temptation to Splurge:

- **Challenge:** The temptation to splurge on non-essential items can test your budgeting discipline.
- **Solution:** Include a category in your budget for discretionary spending. Allow yourself to enjoy occasional splurges within this allocated amount.

4. Overspending:

- **Challenge:** It's easy to overspend in certain categories, leaving less for other financial goals.
- **Solution:** Track your expenses regularly and make necessary adjustments to overspending categories. Use budgeting apps to help you stay within your budget limits.

5. Budget Fatigue:

- **Challenge:** Staying disciplined with budgeting over time can be exhausting.
- **Solution:** Take breaks and celebrate your financial victories. Use rewards and incentives to stay motivated.

6. Irregular Income:

- **Challenge:** Irregular income can make it difficult to create a traditional monthly budget.
- **Solution:** Create a budget based on your average monthly income. When you have a surplus, allocate it to savings or debt repayment.

7. Impulse Buying:

- **Challenge:** Impulse purchases can quickly derail your budget.

- **Solution:** Implement a "cooling-off" period for non-essential purchases. Wait a day or more before making impulsive buys to determine if they align with your financial goals.

8. Inconsistent Tracking:

- **Challenge:** Inconsistent tracking of expenses can lead to budgeting inaccuracies.
- **Solution:** Use budgeting apps or spreadsheets to track expenses regularly. Set a specific day each week or month to review your spending.

9. Not Adjusting for Inflation:

- **Challenge:** Failing to account for inflation can erode your purchasing power over time.
- **Solution:** Periodically adjust your budget for inflation to ensure your financial goals remain achievable.

10. Lack of Emergency Fund:

- **Challenge:** Without an emergency fund, unexpected expenses can lead to debt.
- **Solution:** Build and maintain an emergency fund to provide a financial safety net.

Remember that budgeting is a flexible tool that can adapt to your changing circumstances. It's okay to encounter challenges along the way; what's important is how you address and overcome them. Consistency, adaptability, and patience are key to successful budgeting and achieving your financial goals.

Reward Systems and Celebrating Financial Milestones

Just as sailors find motivation in reaching a port of call, you can find motivation in achieving financial milestones. We'll explore the power of setting up reward systems tied to your goals. Celebrating your achievements—whether it's paying off a credit card, reaching a savings milestone, or sticking to your budget for a set period—can boost your morale and keep you motivated for the journey ahead. By acknowledging your progress, you're reinforcing positive financial behaviors.

1. Define Financial Milestones: Set clear, specific financial milestones. These could include paying off a certain amount of debt, saving for a vacation, or reaching a specific retirement savings target.

2. Attach Rewards to Milestones: Determine rewards that are meaningful to you but won't undermine your financial progress. These could be small treats, experiences, or even a special purchase you've been wanting.

3. Create a Reward System: Establish a system where you "earn" rewards by reaching financial milestones. For example, if you pay off a significant portion of your debt, you could treat yourself to a nice dinner or a spa day.

4. Celebrate Achievements: When you reach a milestone, take time to celebrate. This could involve a small celebration at home, sharing your achievement with friends or family, or even posting about it on social media to hold yourself accountable.

5. Stay Consistent: Incorporate smaller, more frequent rewards for achieving short-term goals to maintain motivation throughout your financial journey.

6. Visual Reminders: Create a visual representation of your financial goals and mark off each milestone as you achieve it. This can be a visual reminder of your progress.

7. Share with Accountability Partners: Share your goals and progress with a trusted friend or family member who can encourage you and help you stay accountable.

8. Adjust and Set New Goals: As you achieve milestones, adjust your goals and set new ones. This keeps you engaged and motivated to continue improving your financial situation.

9. Reflect on Achievements: Take time to reflect on your achievements and express gratitude for your progress. This can reinforce positive financial behaviors and help you stay focused on your goals.

10. Personalize Your Rewards: Choose rewards that resonate with you personally. They don't have to be extravagant; what matters is that they motivate you to reach your goals.

Remember that the journey to financial stability and success is a marathon, not a sprint. Celebrating milestones and using rewards as motivation can make the process more enjoyable and sustainable. It's about finding the right balance between disciplined financial management and enjoying the journey toward your financial goals.

Engaging with a Support Network for Accountability

Accountability can be a powerful force when it comes to maintaining financial discipline. We'll discuss the benefits of engaging with a support network—a group of friends, family members, or like-minded individuals who share your commitment to financial success. By discussing your goals, challenges, and progress with others, you're not only reinforcing your commitment but also benefiting from their insights and encouragement.

1. Accountability Partners: Choose friends, family members, or colleagues who are supportive and can serve as accountability partners.

2. Share Your Goals: Share your financial goals and aspirations with your accountability partners. This opens up an ongoing dialogue about your financial journey.

3. Regular Check-Ins: Set up regular check-in meetings or discussions with your accountability partners. These can be weekly or monthly.

4. Progress Updates: During your meetings, provide updates on your financial progress. Discuss milestones you've reached and any challenges you've encountered.

5. Seek Advice and Guidance: Use these discussions to seek advice and guidance from your accountability network. They may offer valuable insights and solutions to financial challenges.

6. Share Your Challenges: Don't be afraid to share setbacks or obstacles you've faced. Your network can provide emotional support and practical advice.

7. Encouragement and Motivation: Celebrate your achievements together and provide each other with motivation to stay on track.

8. Education and Learning: Explore financial education resources as a group. You can read books, take courses, or attend seminars together to deepen your financial knowledge.

9. Share Resources: Share budgeting apps, tools, or techniques that have worked well for you. Your network may have recommendations that could benefit you as well.

10. Celebrate Successes: Celebrate financial milestones not only individually but also collectively as a group. This reinforces the sense of community and achievement.

11. Be Supportive: Be willing to provide support and

encouragement to your accountability partners in return. It's a mutual exchange.

12. Online Communities: Consider joining online financial communities or forums where you can connect with like-minded individuals who share similar goals and challenges.

Remember that your support network is there to uplift and motivate you on your financial journey. It's a two-way street, and by being an active and supportive member of the network, you can create a positive and empowering environment for everyone involved. Together, you can navigate financial challenges more effectively and work toward shared financial success.

As you navigate the waters of discipline and motivation, remember that this chapter is your compass for staying the course. By overcoming challenges, rewarding your successes, and tapping into the support of others, you're building a strong foundation for a lifelong journey of financial stability and growth. Your dedication to your goals and the strategies you implement to stay on track are the wind in your sails, propelling you toward the financial future you've envisioned.

CHAPTER 9: ADVANCED BUDGETING TECHNIQUES

Your budgeting journey is a continuous evolution, and as you gain experience, you can explore advanced techniques that further optimize your financial strategies. In this chapter, we'll delve into methods for fine-tuning your budget, increasing your income, optimizing expenses, and planning for long-term financial milestones.

Fine-Tuning Your Budget Over Time

A budget is not set in stone—it's a living document that can evolve as your financial situation and goals change. We'll discuss the importance of periodically reviewing and adjusting your budget to reflect your current circumstances. Whether it's a raise at work, a change in living situation, or new financial goals, fine-tuning your budget ensures that it remains a relevant and effective tool on your journey.

Here's how you can effectively adjust your budget as circumstances change:

1. Regular Budget Reviews: Schedule regular budget reviews, ideally monthly or at least quarterly. This allows you to stay on top of your finances and make timely adjustments.

2. Assess Changes in Income: If you receive a raise or a change in income, decide how to allocate the additional funds. Consider increasing savings, investments, or debt payments.

3. Update Expenses: Review your recurring expenses. Are there any subscriptions or services you no longer use or need? Eliminate unnecessary expenses to free up funds.

4. Adjust Financial Goals: When you set new financial goals or adjust existing ones, modify your budget to reflect these changes. Allocate resources toward these objectives.

5. Accommodate Lifestyle Changes: Major life events, such as getting married, having children, or buying a house, require budget adjustments. Factor in new expenses and savings goals.

6. Emergency Fund Maintenance: If you dip into your emergency fund for unexpected expenses, prioritize replenishing it in your budget.

7. Track and Analyze Spending: Continuously track your expenses to ensure they align with your budget. Analyze spending patterns and make adjustments as needed.

8. Savings and Investments: As your financial situation improves, increase contributions to savings accounts, retirement funds, and investments.

9. Debt Management: Adjust your budget to allocate more funds toward debt repayment if your goal is to pay off loans faster.

10. Address Inflation: Periodically adjust your budget to account for inflation, especially if it impacts your essential expenses.

11. Emergency Preparedness: Consider increasing your emergency fund if your circumstances allow, providing additional financial security.

12. Seek Professional Advice: Consult a financial advisor if you're unsure about budget adjustments or if you face complex financial changes.

13. Maintain Flexibility: Remember that a budget should be flexible. Unexpected changes may require quick adjustments, and that's okay.

14. Revisit Long-Term Goals: Periodically review your long-term financial goals, such as retirement planning. Ensure your budget is aligned with these objectives.

By regularly fine-tuning your budget, you not only ensure it remains relevant but also maximize its effectiveness in helping you achieve your financial goals. Be proactive in addressing changes in your income, expenses, and financial aspirations. A well-maintained budget is a powerful tool for financial success.

Strategies for Increasing Income and Optimizing Expenses

To advance financially, it's essential to explore ways to increase your income and optimize your expenses. We'll delve into strategies for generating additional income streams, such as freelancing, consulting, or starting a side business. On the expense side, we'll provide tips for negotiating bills, cutting unnecessary costs, and making mindful spending choices. By maximizing your income and minimizing expenses, you're creating more room in your budget to allocate toward your goals.

Some practical tips for both aspects:

Strategies for Increasing Income:

> **Freelancing or Consulting:** If you have skills or expertise in a particular field, consider freelancing or consulting on the side. You can offer services in areas like writing, graphic design, web development, or consulting in your industry.
> **Side Business:** Start a small side business based on your interests or hobbies. This could include selling handmade crafts, offering tutoring services, or starting an e-commerce store.

Part-Time Work: Look for part-time job opportunities that fit your schedule and skills. Many industries, including retail and hospitality, offer flexible part-time positions.

Passive Income: Explore passive income streams, such as investing in dividend-paying stocks, rental properties, or creating digital products that generate ongoing revenue.

Online Platforms: Utilize online platforms like Upwork, Fiverr, or Etsy to showcase your skills and reach a wider audience.

Strategies for Optimizing Expenses:

Budgeting: Create and stick to a detailed budget. Track your income and expenses to identify areas where you can cut costs.

Negotiate Bills: Contact service providers for your utilities, internet, cable, and insurance to negotiate lower rates or explore better deals.

Eliminate Unnecessary Expenses: Review your monthly expenses and identify non-essential items or subscriptions you can cut, at least temporarily.

Shop Smart: Look for sales, discounts, and use coupons when shopping for groceries, clothing, and other essentials. Consider buying generic brands instead of name brands.

Meal Planning: Plan your meals and cook at home more often to reduce dining out expenses.

Transportation: Explore cost-effective transportation options, like carpooling, biking, or using public transportation, to save on fuel and maintenance costs.

Debt Reduction: Focus on paying down high-interest debts as part of your budget. This not only reduces interest expenses but also frees up more money for saving and investing.

Refinance Loans: Consider refinancing high-interest loans, like student loans or a mortgage, to secure lower interest rates and reduce monthly payments.

Emergency Fund: Maintain an emergency fund to avoid

unexpected expenses derailing your budget.

Mindful Spending: Practice mindful spending by evaluating purchases in terms of necessity and long-term value. Avoid impulse buying.

Comparison Shopping: Before making significant purchases, compare prices from multiple sellers to find the best deal.

Review Subscriptions: Regularly review your subscription services for streaming, fitness, and other memberships. Cancel those you no longer use or need.

Automatic Savings: Set up automatic transfers to your savings or investment accounts as soon as you receive your income.

By implementing these strategies, you can both increase your income and optimize your expenses, ultimately freeing up more funds to achieve your financial goals. It's a comprehensive approach that can significantly improve your financial well-being over time.

Long-Term Financial Planning and Retirement Considerations

While immediate financial goals are essential, it's also crucial to plan for the long term. We'll explore strategies for long-term financial planning, including retirement. We'll discuss the significance of retirement accounts like 401(k)s and IRAs, and how to incorporate retirement savings into your budget. By thinking ahead and making consistent contributions, you're setting the stage for a comfortable and secure retirement.

Here are some key considerations and strategies:

1. Start Early, Compound Growth: The earlier you begin saving for retirement, the more time your investments have to grow through compounding. Even small contributions can make a significant difference over time.

2. Utilize Retirement Accounts:

- **401(k):** If your employer offers a 401(k) plan, take advantage of it. Contribute enough to get any employer match, as it's essentially free money. Maximize your contributions within the annual limits if possible.
- **IRA (Individual Retirement Account):** Consider opening an IRA, either traditional or Roth, depending on your tax situation and retirement goals. IRAs offer tax advantages and a wide range of investment options.

3. Diversify Investments: Diversify your investments across different asset classes, such as stocks, bonds, and real estate, to reduce risk and potentially increase returns.

4. Regularly Review and Adjust: Periodically review your retirement portfolio to ensure it aligns with your long-term goals. Adjust your investments as necessary based on your risk tolerance and changing circumstances.

5. Maximize Contributions: As your income grows or when you receive windfalls (such as bonuses), consider increasing your retirement contributions. Take advantage of catch-up contributions if you're over 50.

6. Plan for Healthcare Costs: Factor in potential healthcare costs in retirement, including Medicare premiums and out-of-pocket expenses. Consider long-term care insurance if needed.

7. Create a Retirement Budget: Estimate your retirement expenses, including housing, utilities, transportation, and leisure activities. Create a retirement budget to ensure you have sufficient income to cover these costs.

8. Social Security Optimization: Determine the optimal age to start receiving Social Security benefits. Delaying can result in larger monthly payments, but the right choice depends on your individual circumstances.

9. Continual Learning: Keep learning about retirement planning, investment strategies, and tax implications. Consider seeking advice from a financial advisor who specializes in retirement planning.

10. Adjust Retirement Age: Be open to the possibility of adjusting your retirement age based on your financial situation. Delaying retirement by a few years can significantly boost your retirement savings.

11. Estate Planning: Include estate planning in your retirement considerations. Decide how you want to distribute your assets and ensure you have appropriate documents, such as a will and power of attorney.

12. Maintain an Emergency Fund: Keep a small emergency fund even in retirement to cover unexpected expenses without disrupting your retirement savings.

Long-term financial planning for retirement requires consistent effort and a strategic approach. By saving diligently, investing wisely, and staying informed about your financial options, you can work towards a comfortable and secure retirement that aligns with your goals and aspirations.

As you explore advanced budgeting techniques, remember that this chapter is about refining your skills and strategies. By fine-tuning your budget over time, increasing your income, optimizing expenses, and planning for long-term financial milestones, you're demonstrating your commitment to ongoing financial growth and stability. Your willingness to adapt and innovate ensures that your financial journey remains dynamic and aligned with your aspirations.

CHAPTER 10: BEYOND BUDGETING – FINANCIAL FREEDOM

Congratulations, you've mastered the art of budgeting! But your journey doesn't end here; it's just the beginning of a life enriched with financial freedom and empowerment. In this final chapter, we'll explore how to take your financial success beyond budgeting, creating a legacy of prosperity and impact.

Achieving Financial Goals Beyond Budgeting

Budgeting has equipped you with the tools to achieve your initial financial goals, but now it's time to dream bigger. We'll discuss strategies for setting more ambitious objectives—whether it's early retirement, travel adventures, or starting a philanthropic endeavor. By leveraging the financial foundation you've built through budgeting, you're positioned to pursue aspirations that were once considered out of reach.

1. Define Your Big Financial Goals: Clearly define your larger financial objectives. This might include early retirement, world travel, starting a business, or significant philanthropic contributions.

2. Create a Plan: Break down your big goals into smaller, actionable steps. Determine what you need to achieve at various points along the way.

3. Continue Budgeting: Continue budgeting, but adjust your budget to accommodate your larger goals. Allocate a portion of your income specifically to these objectives.

4. Invest Strategically: Consider more advanced investment strategies to grow your wealth, such as investing in stocks, bonds, real estate, or alternative investments.

5. Explore Passive Income Streams: Look into passive income opportunities, such as dividend-paying stocks, rental properties, or creating digital products that generate ongoing income.

6. Review and Adjust: Periodically review your progress toward your big goals. Adjust your plan and budget as needed based on your achievements and changing circumstances.

7. Seek Expert Advice: Consult with a financial advisor who specializes in advanced financial planning to optimize your strategy.

8. Continuous Learning: Stay informed about advanced financial concepts and strategies to make informed decisions about your investments and wealth growth.

9. Risk Management: Understand the risks associated with your larger financial goals and have a risk management plan in place to protect your wealth.

10. Philanthropy and Giving: If philanthropy is part of your aspirations, explore ways to contribute to causes you care about. This might involve setting up a charitable foundation or participating in impactful philanthropic projects.

11. Build a Legacy: Consider how you want to leave a legacy for future generations. Estate planning can help ensure your wealth is distributed according to your wishes.

12. Enjoy the Journey: While pursuing ambitious financial goals is important, remember to balance your efforts with enjoying life along the way. Achieving these goals should enhance your quality of life, not detract from it.

By setting and working towards more ambitious financial goals, you can use your budgeting skills as a strong foundation to make your dreams a reality. These goals may require more time and effort, but with dedication and a well-thought-out plan, you can achieve financial success beyond your initial expectations.

Creating a Sustainable and Prosperous Financial Future

A sustainable financial future is built on principles of balance and responsible stewardship. We'll delve into the importance of maintaining the habits you've developed, like tracking expenses and living within your means. We'll also explore how to invest wisely, protect your assets, and make informed financial decisions that contribute to long-term prosperity.

Key principles to consider:

1. Continuous Budgeting: Budgeting isn't just a one-time task; it's a lifelong practice. Continue tracking expenses, setting financial goals, and living within your means.

2. Emergency Fund Maintenance: Keep your emergency fund well-funded to handle unexpected expenses and financial setbacks.

3. Investment Strategy: Maintain a diversified investment portfolio that aligns with your risk tolerance and long-term goals. Regularly review and rebalance your investments.

4. Risk Management: Ensure you have appropriate insurance coverage, including health, life, and property insurance, to protect your assets and loved ones.

5. Estate Planning: Update your estate plan as needed to ensure your assets are distributed according to your wishes. Consider the impact of taxes on your estate.

6. Financial Education: Stay informed about financial matters and investment opportunities. Attend workshops, read books, or take courses to enhance your financial knowledge.

7. Sustainable Living: Consider sustainable and environmentally responsible choices in your daily life. This can include energy-efficient home upgrades, responsible consumption, and ethical investing.

8. Charitable Giving: Continue supporting causes you care about through charitable giving. Consider creating a charitable foundation or donor-advised fund for more significant contributions.

9. Retirement Planning: Regularly review your retirement plan and adjust contributions as necessary. Keep your retirement goals in focus.

10. Avoid Debt: Continue managing debt wisely and avoid accumulating unnecessary debt. Focus on paying off high-interest debts.

11. Healthy Lifestyle: A healthy lifestyle can lead to lower healthcare costs and a higher quality of life in retirement.

12. Review and Reflect: Periodically review your financial situation and goals. Reflect on your progress and adjust your strategy as needed.

13. Seek Professional Advice: Consider consulting a financial advisor to fine-tune your financial plan and ensure you're on track for long-term prosperity.

14. Financial Independence: If early retirement is a goal, plan for financial independence. Explore strategies like the 4% rule to determine how much you need to retire comfortably.

15. Enjoy Life: While financial planning is essential, don't forget to enjoy life along the way. Find a balance that allows you to savor the present while preparing for the future.

Building a sustainable and prosperous financial future is a lifelong journey that requires discipline, ongoing education, and a commitment to responsible financial stewardship. By following these principles and staying focused on your goals, you can achieve financial security and enjoy the fruits of your efforts in the years to come.

Building Wealth and Giving Back to Your Community

True financial success isn't just about accumulating wealth—it's about making a positive impact. We'll discuss how to use your financial stability to give back to your community and support causes you care about. Whether it's through charitable donations, volunteer work, or investing in local initiatives, you have the power to create meaningful change beyond your personal finances.

ways to give back and support causes you care about:

1. Charitable Giving:

- **Regular Donations:** Allocate a portion of your income for regular charitable donations to organizations and causes you believe in.
- **Donor-Advised Funds:** Consider setting up a donor-advised fund that allows you to make tax-deductible contributions and recommend grants to charities over time.

2. Volunteer Work: Contribute your time and skills to local charities and nonprofits. Volunteering can be just as valuable as financial donations.

3. Impact Investing: Consider impact investing, which involves investing in companies and funds that align with your values and have a positive societal or environmental impact.

4. Support Local Initiatives: Support local businesses, as they often play a crucial role in community development.

- **Community Projects:** Invest in community projects, such as parks, schools, or cultural institutions, that enhance the quality of life in your area.

5. Educational Initiatives: Establish scholarships or educational programs to support local students pursuing higher education.

6. Mentorship: Offer mentorship or coaching to individuals looking to improve their financial literacy or career prospects.

7. Environmental Stewardship: Invest in environmental projects that promote sustainability and protect natural resources.

8. Collaborate with Others: Partner with like-minded individuals or organizations to pool resources and have a more significant impact on the causes you care about.

9. Legacy Planning: Consider including charitable bequests in your estate plan to ensure your wealth continues to support your chosen causes even after your passing.

10. Measuring Impact: Regularly evaluate the impact of your financial contributions and efforts to ensure they align with your goals and make a meaningful difference.

11. Raise Awareness: Use your financial stability and influence to advocate for social and economic issues that matter to you.

Remember that giving back and supporting your community can be immensely fulfilling. It allows you to use your financial success as a force for positive change, creating a legacy of impact that extends beyond your personal wealth.

As you step into the realm of financial freedom, remember that this chapter represents the culmination of your journey. By achieving financial goals beyond budgeting, creating a sustainable and prosperous financial future, and embracing the opportunity to give back, you're embarking on a path of significance and fulfillment. Your dedication to mastering budgeting has set the stage for a life of empowerment, impact, and lasting financial well-being.

CONCLUSION:

As you reach the end of this transformative journey through the world of budgeting, take a moment to reflect on how far you've come. From a budgeting beginner, you've emerged as a financial master, equipped with the knowledge, skills, and strategies to shape your financial destiny. Your commitment to learning, planning, and discipline has brought you to this point, and the path ahead is filled with promise.

Remember that the journey doesn't end here. Just as life is dynamic, so too is your financial situation. As you continue your path, embrace the idea of constant refinement and adaptation. Your budget, which once might have felt like a daunting task, has become a tool that empowers you to achieve your goals, manage challenges, and create a life of financial stability and freedom.

The newfound financial confidence you've gained is invaluable. It's not just about numbers on a spreadsheet—it's about the choices you make, the dreams you pursue, and the legacy you leave. By mastering budgeting, you've unlocked the door to a brighter future—one where you're in control of your money, rather than the other way around.

So, as you journey forward, embrace the lessons you've learned, the habits you've cultivated, and the goals you've set. Keep adapting, keep learning, and keep dreaming. The financial mastery you've achieved is a testament to your dedication and perseverance. You've built a foundation that supports your aspirations, and the possibilities that lie ahead are boundless.

Congratulations on your journey from budgeting beginner to financial mastery. Your future is as bright as your determination to shape it.

APPENDIX A: BUDGETING TEMPLATES AND WORKSHEETS

To assist you in your budgeting endeavors, we've compiled a selection of templates and worksheets that cater to various aspects of your financial planning. These resources are designed to make the process smoother and more organized, helping you take control of your finances with confidence.

Monthly Budget Template: A comprehensive template for creating a monthly budget, allowing you to allocate income to various expense categories:

Income:

Primary Job: $
Side Gig/Part-Time Job: $
Rental Income: $
Freelance Work: $
Investment Income: $
Other Income (e.g., gifts, bonuses): $
Total Income: $

Expenses:

Fixed Expenses:

Rent/Mortgage: $
Utilities (Electricity, Water, Gas, Internet, etc.): $
Insurance (Health, Auto, Home, Life, etc.): $
Loan Payments (Car, Student Loans, etc.): $
Subscriptions (Netflix, Gym, etc.): $
Total Fixed Expenses: $

Variable Expenses:

Groceries: $
Transportation (Gas, Public Transit, etc.): $
Dining Out: $
Entertainment (Movies, Concerts, etc.): $
Shopping (Clothes, Electronics, etc.): $
Total Variable Expenses: $

Discretionary Expenses:

Gifts/Donations: $
Personal Care (Haircuts, Toiletries, etc.): $
Hobbies/Leisure Activities: $
Travel/Vacation: $
Miscellaneous: $
Total Discretionary Expenses: $

Non-Discretionary Expenses:

Health (Medications, Doctor Visits, etc.): $
Groceries (if partially discretionary): $
Utilities (if partially discretionary): $
Total Non-Discretionary Expenses: $

Savings and Investments:

Emergency Fund: $
Retirement Accounts (401(k), IRA, etc.): $
Other Savings Goals (Vacation Fund, Home Down Payment, etc.):
$
Total Savings and Investments: $

Debt Repayment:

Credit Card 1: $
Credit Card 2: $
Student Loans: $
Other Loans: $
Total Debt Repayment: $

Total Expenses:

Net Income (Income - Total Expenses):

Budget Summary:

Savings Rate (Savings/Income x 100): %
Debt-to-Income Ratio (Total Debt Payments/Income x 100): %
Budget Variance (Net Income - 0): $

Notes:

- Customize the template by adding or removing expense categories based on your financial situation.
- Assign specific dollar amounts to each expense category, ensuring they add up to your total income.
- Periodically review and adjust your budget as needed to reflect changes in your income or expenses.
- Use budgeting software or apps to track your spending and stay on top of your financial goals.

Expense Tracking Worksheet: A tool to record your daily expenses and track where your money is going.

Date:

Expense Category: (e.g., Groceries, Transportation, Dining Out, Entertainment, etc.)

Date	Expense Description	Amount ($)
[Date]	[Description]	[Amount]
[Date]	[Description]	[Amount]
[Date]	[Description]	[Amount]
[Date]	[Description]	[Amount]
[Date]	[Description]	[Amount]
[Date]	[Description]	[Amount]
[Date]	[Description]	[Amount]
[Date]	[Description]	[Amount]
[Date]	[Description]	[Amount]
[Date]	[Description]	[Amount]

[Date]	[Description]	[Amount]
[Date]	[Description]	[Amount]
[Date]	[Description]	[Amount]
[Date]	[Description]	[Amount]
[Date]	[Description]	[Amount]
[Date]	[Description]	[Amount]
[Date]	[Description]	[Amount]
[Date]	[Description]	[Amount]
[Date]	[Description]	[Amount]
[Date]	[Description]	[Amount]
[Date]	[Description]	[Amount]
[Date]	[Description]	[Amount]
[Date]	[Description]	[Amount]
[Date]	[Description]	[Amount]
[Date]	[Description]	[Amount]
[Date]	[Description]	[Amount]

Total Daily Expenses: $

Expense Tracking Tips:

Record Every Expense: Make it a habit to record every expense, no matter how small. This ensures accuracy in tracking your spending.

Use Categories: Categorize expenses (e.g., groceries, transportation, entertainment) to identify spending patterns.

Be Specific: Include details about each expense, such as where and why you spent the money.

Keep Receipts: Save receipts and attach them to your worksheet whenever possible for reference.

Daily or Weekly Review: Review your expenses daily or weekly to stay on top of your budget and identify areas where you may need to cut back.

Stay Consistent: Consistency is key to effective expense tracking. Stick to the practice even when it feels tedious.

Use Apps: Consider using budgeting apps or software to streamline the process and generate reports for better insights into your spending.

Debt Payoff Tracker: A worksheet to visualize and track your progress in paying off different debts.

Debt Name: [Name of the Debt]

Initial Debt Balance: $[Initial Balance]

Monthly Payment: $[Monthly Payment]

Interest Rate: [Interest Rate %]

Payment Due Date: [Due Date]

Month	Starting Balance ($)	Monthly Payment ($)	Interest ($)	Principal Payment ($)	Ending Balance ($)

[Month 1]	[Initial Balance]	[Monthly Payment]	[Interest]	[Principal Payment]	[Ending Balance]
[Month 2]	[Ending Balance]	[Monthly Payment]	[Interest]	[Principal Payment]	[Ending Balance]
[Month 3]	[Ending Balance]	[Monthly Payment]	[Interest]	[Principal Payment]	[Ending Balance]
[Month 4]	[Ending Balance]	[Monthly Payment]	[Interest]	[Principal Payment]	[Ending Balance]
[Month 5]	[Ending Balance]	[Monthly Payment]	[Interest]	[Principal Payment]	[Ending Balance]
[Month 6]	[Ending Balance]	[Monthly Payment]	[Interest]	[Principal Payment]	[Ending Balance]
[Month 7]	[Ending Balance]	[Monthly Payment]	[Interest]	[Principal Payment]	[Ending Balance]
[Month 8]	[Ending Balance]	[Monthly Payment]	[Interest]	[Principal Payment]	[Ending Balance]
[Month 9]	[Ending Balance]	[Monthly Payment]	[Interest]	[Principal Payment]	[Ending Balance]
[Month 10]	[Ending Balance]	[Monthly Payment]	[Interest]	[Principal Payment]	[Ending Balance]
[Month 11]	[Ending Balance]	[Monthly Payment]	[Interest]	[Principal Payment]	[Ending Balance]
[Month 12]	[Ending Balance]	[Monthly Payment]	[Interest]	[Principal Payment]	[Ending Balance]

Total Interest Paid: $[Total Interest Paid]

Projected Payoff Date: [Payoff Date]

Debt Payoff Tips:

- Always pay more than the minimum payment when possible to accelerate your debt payoff.
- Consider the debt snowball or debt avalanche method to decide which debt to pay off first.
- Stay consistent with your monthly payments, even if they are higher than the minimum required.
- Celebrate milestones along the way to stay motivated.
- Adjust your budget to allocate extra funds towards debt repayment when you can.

By using this debt payoff tracker, you can visually see your progress over time, which can be a powerful motivator as you work towards becoming debt-free. Remember to update it each month to stay on top of your repayment plan and celebrate your achievements along the way.

Savings Goal Worksheet: A worksheet to outline your savings goals, set target dates, and track your progress.

Savings Goal: [Description of Your Savings Goal]

Target Amount: $[Target Amount]

Target Date: [Target Date]

Starting Balance: $[Starting Balance, if applicable]

Monthly Contribution: $[Monthly Contribution]

Month	Starting Balance ($)	Monthly Contribution ($)	Ending Balance ($)
[Month 1]	[Starting Balance]	[Monthly Contribution]	[Ending Balance]

[Month 2]	[Ending Balance]	[Monthly Contribution]	[Ending Balance]
[Month 3]	[Ending Balance]	[Monthly Contribution]	[Ending Balance]
[Month 4]	[Ending Balance]	[Monthly Contribution]	[Ending Balance]
[Month 5]	[Ending Balance]	[Monthly Contribution]	[Ending Balance]
[Month 6]	[Ending Balance]	[Monthly Contribution]	[Ending Balance]
[Month 7]	[Ending Balance]	[Monthly Contribution]	[Ending Balance]
[Month 8]	[Ending Balance]	[Monthly Contribution]	[Ending Balance]
[Month 9]	[Ending Balance]	[Monthly Contribution]	[Ending Balance]
[Month 10]	[Ending Balance]	[Monthly Contribution]	[Ending Balance]
[Month 11]	[Ending Balance]	[Monthly Contribution]	[Ending Balance]
[Month 12]	[Ending Balance]	[Monthly Contribution]	[Ending Balance]

Total Contributions: $[Total Contributions]

Total Interest Earned: $[Total Interest Earned, if applicable]

Actual Completion Date: [Actual Completion Date, if achieved]

Savings Goal Tips:

- Set specific, measurable, achievable, relevant, and time-bound (SMART) goals to clarify your objectives.
- Determine how much you need to save each month to reach your target by the set date.
- Consider opening a dedicated savings account for each goal to avoid mixing funds.
- Regularly review your progress and adjust contributions as needed based on changes in your financial situation.

Use this savings goal worksheet for each financial goal you have, whether it's saving for an emergency fund, a vacation, a down payment on a house, or any other objective. It can help you stay organized, motivated, and on track as you work towards achieving your financial aspirations.

Emergency Fund Tracker: Use this tracker to monitor your emergency fund's growth and ensure you're prepared for unexpected expenses.

Emergency Fund Goal: $[Your Emergency Fund Goal]

Starting Balance: $[Initial Balance]

Month	Starting Balance ($)	Monthly Contribution ($)	Interest Earned ($)	Ending Balance ($)
[Month 1]	[Initial Balance]	[Monthly Contribution]	[Interest Earned]	[Ending Balance]

[Month 2]	[Ending Balance]	[Monthly Contribution]	[Interest Earned]	[Ending Balance]
[Month 3]	[Ending Balance]	[Monthly Contribution]	[Interest Earned]	[Ending Balance]
[Month 4]	[Ending Balance]	[Monthly Contribution]	[Interest Earned]	[Ending Balance]
[Month 5]	[Ending Balance]	[Monthly Contribution]	[Interest Earned]	[Ending Balance]
[Month 6]	[Ending Balance]	[Monthly Contribution]	[Interest Earned]	[Ending Balance]
[Month 7]	[Ending Balance]	[Monthly Contribution]	[Interest Earned]	[Ending Balance]
[Month 8]	[Ending Balance]	[Monthly Contribution]	[Interest Earned]	[Ending Balance]
[Month 9]	[Ending Balance]	[Monthly Contribution]	[Interest Earned]	[Ending Balance]
[Month 10]	[Ending Balance]	[Monthly Contribution]	[Interest Earned]	[Ending Balance]
[Month 11]	[Ending Balance]	[Monthly Contribution]	[Interest Earned]	[Ending Balance]
[Month 12]	[Ending Balance]	[Monthly Contribution]	[Interest Earned]	[Ending Balance]

Total Contributions: $[Total Contributions]

Total Interest Earned: $[Total Interest Earned]

Projected Completion Date: [Projected Completion Date]

Emergency Fund Tips:

- Set a specific savings goal for your emergency fund to give you a clear target to work towards.
- Make automatic monthly contributions to your emergency fund to ensure consistent progress.
- Consider using a high-yield savings account to earn more interest on your savings.
- Avoid using the emergency fund for non-emergencies to maintain its purpose.
- Adjust your monthly contributions as your financial situation improves.

This emergency fund tracker allows you to visualize your progress and stay motivated as you build a financial safety net for unexpected expenses. Be diligent in updating it regularly, and remember that having an adequate emergency fund can provide peace of mind and financial security.

Income and Expense Summary: An overview of your monthly income and expenses, providing insight into your financial health.

Income:

Salary/Wages: $[Monthly Salary/Wages]
Rental Income: $[Monthly Rental Income, if applicable]
Side Gig Income: $[Monthly Side Gig Income, if applicable]
Freelance Income: $[Monthly Freelance Income, if applicable]
Investment Income: $[Monthly Investment Income, if applicable]
Other Income: $[Other Monthly Income, if applicable]
Total Monthly Income: $[Total Monthly Income]

Expenses:

Fixed Expenses:
- Rent/Mortgage: $[Monthly Rent/Mortgage Payment]
- Utilities: $[Monthly Utilities Expenses]
- Insurance (Auto, Health, etc.): $[Monthly Insurance Expenses]
- Loan Payments (e.g., Student Loans, Car Loans): $[Total Monthly Loan Payments]
- Other Fixed Expenses: $[Total Other Fixed Expenses]

Variable Expenses:
- Groceries: $[Monthly Groceries Expenses]
- Transportation (Gas, Public Transport): $[Monthly Transportation Expenses]
- Dining Out: $[Monthly Dining Out Expenses]
- Entertainment: $[Monthly Entertainment Expenses]
- Clothing: $[Monthly Clothing Expenses]
- Personal Care (Toiletries, Health Expenses): $[Monthly Personal Care Expenses]
- Other Variable Expenses: $[Total Other Variable Expenses]

Savings and Investments:
- Emergency Fund Contribution: $[Monthly Emergency Fund Contribution]
- Retirement Account Contribution: $[Monthly Retirement Account Contribution]
- Other Savings/Investment Contributions: $[Total Other Savings/Investment Contributions]

Debt Payments:
- Credit Card Payments: $[Monthly Credit Card Payments]
- Loan Payments (e.g., Personal Loans): $[Monthly Loan Payments]
- Other Debt Payments: $[Total Other Debt Payments]

Total Monthly Expenses: $[Total Monthly Expenses]

Net Income (Income - Expenses): $[Net Monthly Income]

Income and Expense Analysis:

- Compare your total monthly income to your total monthly expenses to assess your financial health.
- Calculate your net income (income minus expenses) to understand how much discretionary income you have.
- Consider reviewing and adjusting your budget regularly to align your spending with your financial goals.

This income and expense summary provides a snapshot of your financial situation, helping you see where your money is coming from and where it's going. Use it to make informed decisions about budgeting, savings, and financial goals.

Yearly Budget Planner: Plan your budget for the entire year, accounting for annual expenses and varying income sources.

Income:

Salary/Wages: $[Monthly Salary/Wages] x 12 months
Rental Income: $[Monthly Rental Income, if applicable] x 12 months
Side Gig Income: $[Monthly Side Gig Income, if applicable] x 12 months
Freelance Income: $[Monthly Freelance Income, if applicable] x 12 months
Investment Income: $[Monthly Investment Income, if applicable] x 12 months
Other Income: $[Other Monthly Income, if applicable] x 12 months
Total Yearly Income: $[Total Yearly Income]

Expenses:

Fixed Expenses:

- Rent/Mortgage: $[Monthly Rent/Mortgage Payment] x 12 months
- Utilities: $[Monthly Utilities Expenses] x 12 months
- Insurance (Auto, Health, etc.): $[Monthly Insurance Expenses] x 12 months
- Loan Payments (e.g., Student Loans, Car Loans): $[Total Monthly Loan Payments] x 12 months
- Other Fixed Expenses: $[Total Other Fixed Expenses] x 12 months

Variable Expenses:

- Groceries: $[Monthly Groceries Expenses] x 12 months
- Transportation (Gas, Public Transport): $[Monthly Transportation Expenses] x 12 months
- Dining Out: $[Monthly Dining Out Expenses] x 12 months
- Entertainment: $[Monthly Entertainment Expenses] x 12 months
- Clothing: $[Monthly Clothing Expenses] x 12 months
- Personal Care (Toiletries, Health Expenses): $[Monthly Personal Care Expenses] x 12 months
- Other Variable Expenses: $[Total Other Variable Expenses] x 12 months

Savings and Investments:

- Emergency Fund Contribution: $[Monthly Emergency Fund Contribution] x 12 months
- Retirement Account Contribution: $[Monthly Retirement Account Contribution] x 12 months
- Other Savings/Investment Contributions: $[Total Other Savings/Investment Contributions] x 12 months

Debt Payments:

- Credit Card Payments: $[Monthly Credit Card Payments] x 12 months
- Loan Payments (e.g., Personal Loans): $[Monthly Loan Payments] x 12 months
- Other Debt Payments: $[Total Other Debt Payments] x 12 months

Total Yearly Expenses: $[Total Yearly Expenses]

Net Income (Income - Expenses): $[Net Yearly Income]

Yearly Budget Analysis:

- Use this yearly budget planner to account for both monthly and annual expenses.
- Calculate your net yearly income (yearly income minus yearly expenses) to assess your overall financial health.
- Consider allocating funds for annual expenses (e.g., insurance premiums, property taxes) into a dedicated savings account to ensure you have the funds when needed.

This yearly budget planner allows you to take a comprehensive view of your finances for the entire year, making it easier to plan for both regular monthly expenses and occasional annual costs. Use it to stay organized and make informed financial decisions throughout the year.

Investment Tracking Sheet: Keep track of your investments, including stocks, bonds, mutual funds, and other assets.

Investment Account Information:

Account Name: [Name of the Investment Account]
Account Number: [Account Number, if applicable]
Financial Institution: [Name of the Financial Institution]
Account Type: [e.g., Brokerage Account, IRA, 401(k)]

Investment Portfolio:

Asset Name	Ticker Symbol	Quantity	Purchase Date	Purchase Price per Unit	Current Price per Unit	Market Value	Gain/ Loss
[Asset 1]	[Ticker 1]	[Quantity]	[Purchase Date]	$ [Purchase Price]	$[Current Price]	$[Market Value]	$[Gain/ Loss]
[Asset 2]	[Ticker 2]	[Quantity]	[Purchase Date]	$ [Purchase Price]	$[Current Price]	$[Market Value]	$[Gain/ Loss]
...	...	...	...	...	...	...	...

Total Portfolio Value: $[Total Portfolio Value]

Investment Summary:

Total Investment Value: $[Total Portfolio Value]
Total Gain/Loss: $[Total Gain/Loss]
Investment Return (ROI): [ROI Calculation]
Notes: [Any additional notes or comments about your investments]

Investment Tracking Tips:

- Update your investment tracking sheet regularly to reflect changes in asset prices and quantities.
- Consider categorizing your investments by asset class (e.g., stocks, bonds, mutual funds) for better organization.
- Calculate the gain/loss for each asset by subtracting the purchase price from the current price.
- Monitor your portfolio's performance and make informed investment decisions based on your goals and risk tolerance.

Use this investment tracking sheet to gain a clear overview of your investment portfolio and make informed decisions about your investment strategy. It can help you track your progress toward financial goals and assess the performance of your investments over time.

Retirement Planning Worksheet: Calculate how much you need to save for retirement and plan your contributions accordingly.

Current Financial Situation:

Current Age: [Your Current Age]
Desired Retirement Age: [Age at Which You Want to Retire]
Life Expectancy: [Your Estimated Life Expectancy]
Current Annual Income: $[Your Current Annual Income]
Current Retirement Savings: $[Your Current Retirement Savings]
Expected Social Security Income: $[Estimated Social Security Income]

Retirement Goals:

Desired Retirement Lifestyle: [Describe Your Desired Lifestyle in Retirement]
Retirement Income Replacement Rate: [Percentage of Current Income You Want to Replace in Retirement, e.g., 80%]

Estimated Retirement Expenses:

Annual Retirement Expenses: $[Estimated Annual Expenses in Retirement]

Retirement Savings Target:

Total Retirement Savings Needed: $[Estimated Total Savings Needed for Retirement]

Calculate this by multiplying your annual retirement expenses by the number of years in retirement (life expectancy minus retirement age).

Retirement Contributions:

Years Until Retirement: [Number of Years Until Desired Retirement Age]
Annual Retirement Savings Goal: $[Annual Savings Goal]

Calculate this by dividing your total retirement savings needed by the number of years until retirement.

Sources of Retirement Income:

Expected Social Security Income: $[Estimated Social Security Income]
Expected Income from Current Savings: $[Expected Income from Current Savings]

Calculate this by estimating the income generated by your current retirement savings based on a safe withdrawal rate (e.g., 4%).

Additional Retirement Savings Needed:

Annual Shortfall: $[Annual Shortfall]

Calculate this by subtracting your expected retirement income (Social Security + income from current savings) from your annual retirement expenses.

Retirement Savings Strategy:

Monthly Retirement Savings Goal: $[Monthly Savings Goal]

Calculate this by dividing your annual savings goal by 12 months.

Retirement Contribution Plan:

Current Monthly Retirement Contributions: $[Your Current Monthly Contributions]
Additional Monthly Contributions Needed: $[Additional Monthly Contributions Needed to Meet Your Goal]
Calculate this by subtracting your current monthly contributions from your monthly savings goal.

Retirement Planning Tips:

- Regularly review and adjust your retirement planning worksheet as your financial situation changes.
- Consider consulting a financial advisor for personalized retirement planning guidance.
- Explore retirement account options (e.g., 401(k), IRA) and take advantage of employer matches if available.
- Maximize tax-advantaged retirement contributions to boost your savings.

This retirement planning worksheet serves as a roadmap for estimating your retirement needs and determining how much you should save each month to reach your retirement goals. By following this plan and making regular contributions, you can work towards achieving a comfortable retirement.

Net Worth Calculator: Assess your net worth by subtracting your liabilities from your assets, helping you gauge your overall financial position.

Assets:

Cash and Bank Accounts: $[Total Cash and Bank Accounts]
Investment Accounts (e.g., brokerage accounts, retirement accounts): $[Total Investment Accounts]
Real Estate (e.g., home value, rental property): $[Total Real Estate Value]
Vehicles (e.g., car value): $[Total Vehicle Value]
Other Assets (e.g., jewelry, collectibles): $[Total Other Assets]
Total Assets: $[Total Assets]

Liabilities (Debts):

Mortgage: $[Mortgage Balance]
Auto Loans: $[Auto Loan Balance]
Credit Card Debt: $[Total Credit Card Debt]
Student Loans: $[Total Student Loan Debt]
Other Loans (e.g., personal loans): $[Total Other Loan Debt]
Total Liabilities (Total Debts): $[Total Liabilities]

Net Worth Calculation:

Total Assets: $[Total Assets]
Total Liabilities (Total Debts): $[Total Liabilities]
Net Worth (Assets - Liabilities): $[Net Worth]

Net Worth Analysis:

- Your current net worth is an indicator of your financial health. A positive net worth means your assets exceed your debts, while a negative net worth indicates the opposite.
- Regularly track your net worth to measure your financial progress over time.
- Setting financial goals and reducing debt can help increase your net worth.

Use this net worth calculator to evaluate your financial situation periodically and make informed decisions about your finances. It provides a clear snapshot of your wealth by calculating the difference between what you own (assets) and what you owe (liabilities).

Remember that these templates and worksheets are adaptable to your specific needs and goals. You can use them as-is or modify them to suit your preferences. By utilizing these resources, you're taking a proactive step towards understanding your finances and achieving your financial objectives.

APPENDIX B: RECOMMENDED APPS AND TOOLS FOR BUDGETING

In today's digital age, there's a plethora of apps and tools designed to make budgeting more convenient and efficient. These tools can help you track expenses, manage your budget, and gain valuable insights into your financial habits. Here are some of the top recommended apps and tools for budgeting:

Mint: An all-in-one budgeting app that aggregates your financial accounts, tracks expenses, and provides personalized budget recommendations.

You Need a Budget (YNAB): YNAB uses a unique approach to budgeting, focusing on giving every dollar a job and helping users prioritize their spending.

PocketGuard: This app offers a clear view of your financial situation, tracks spending, and helps you set up budget categories based on your income and goals.

Goodbudget: Inspired by the envelope budgeting system, Goodbudget lets you allocate funds to virtual envelopes for different spending categories.

EveryDollar: Created by financial expert Dave Ramsey, EveryDollar helps you create a zero-based budget and stay on top of your finances.

Personal Capital: While primarily known for investment tracking, Personal Capital also provides budgeting tools to help you manage your finances holistically.

Wally: Wally is designed for expense tracking, allowing you to capture receipts and monitor your spending habits.

Simple: This app combines budgeting and banking, offering a checking account with budgeting tools that automatically categorize your spending.

PocketSmith: With forecasting features, PocketSmith helps you plan for future expenses, savings goals, and financial milestones.

Expensify: Primarily for business-related expenses, Expensify can also be used for personal expense tracking and reporting.

These apps and tools can streamline your budgeting process, offering convenience and insights to help you manage your money effectively. As you explore these options, consider your preferences and the features that align with your budgeting style and goals.

APPENDIX C: ADDITIONAL RESOURCES FOR FURTHER LEARNING ABOUT PERSONAL FINANCE

Your journey to financial mastery is a continuous process of learning and growth. To expand your knowledge and deepen your understanding of personal finance, consider exploring these additional resources:

Books:

"The Total Money Makeover" by Dave Ramsey: A comprehensive guide to personal finance, covering budgeting, debt reduction, and building wealth.

"The Millionaire Next Door" by Thomas J. Stanley and William D. Danko: Explores the habits and characteristics of ordinary people who have achieved financial success.

"Rich Dad Poor Dad" by Robert T. Kiyosaki: Offers valuable insights into financial literacy, investing, and building wealth.

"Your Money or Your Life" by Vicki Robin and Joe Dominguez: A transformative book that challenges conventional ideas about money and offers a path toward financial independence.

Websites and Blogs:

Investopedia: A comprehensive resource for learning about various financial topics, from investing and budgeting to retirement planning and more.

The Balance: Offers a wide range of articles and guides on personal finance, including budgeting strategies, saving tips, and investing advice.

Bogleheads: A community focused on the principles of John C. Bogle, founder of Vanguard, known for his passive investing philosophy.

Mr. Money Mustache: A blog that emphasizes early retirement, financial independence, and frugal living.

Podcasts:

The Dave Ramsey Show: Offers practical advice on budgeting, debt reduction, and achieving financial goals.

Afford Anything: Hosted by Paula Pant, this podcast explores topics like real estate, investing, and achieving financial freedom.

ChooseFI: Explores the path to financial independence through interviews and discussions on various personal finance strategies.

The Clark Howard Podcast: Covers a wide range of financial topics, from consumer advice to saving money on everyday expenses.

Online Courses:

Coursera: Offers a variety of online courses on personal finance, investing, and financial planning.

Udemy: Provides courses on budgeting, investing, and other financial topics taught by experts in the field.

Khan Academy: Offers free courses on personal finance, investing, and economics, suitable for learners of all levels.

These resources provide a wealth of information to support your ongoing journey toward financial literacy and success. Remember that the more you learn and apply, the more empowered you become in making informed financial decisions that align with your goals and aspirations.

As you explore these appendices, remember that they're here to serve as your ongoing toolkit for success. Whether you're seeking practical tools for budgeting, recommendations for budgeting apps, or opportunities to expand your financial knowledge, these resources are at your disposal to support your continued growth on your financial journey.